ART NOUVE

Poems Old and New
Jane Davis Carpenter

ART NOUVEAU DREAMS

TABLE OF CONTENTS

ACKNOWLEDGMENTS

Some of the poems contained herein were written under a grant from Rocky Mountain Women's Institute. I thank RMWI for their strong support. Three writers' groups have been highly motivating: The National League of American Pen Women; National Writers' Association, Denver Metro Chapter, and The Poetry Society of Colorado, Inc.

A number of publications, both mainstream and literary, have published my work: *The New York Times, The Denver Post, Good Housekeeping, Woman's Day, Visions, Salomé, Pandora, Blue Unicorn*, and the Pen Women anthology, *Collage*.

Cover art by Elizabeth A. Gasper:
ceramic sculpture, "Art Nouveau Dreams"

LIBRARY OF CONGRESS CATALOGING IN PUBLICATION DATA

Carpenter, Jane Davis

Art Nouveau Dreams–Poems 1948-1998 / Jane Davis Carpenter (1998)

Jane Davis Carpenter

THE VOICES

They call to us from out the past;
　Their whistles stir the soul
With what a mesmerizing blast!
　Now miles of track unroll,
Configuration to be crossed
　Like complex silver webs—
And yet no time is ever lost;
　The fluxes balance ebbs.

The paradiddle of the chuffs
　Can parody snare drums
As engine climbs to steeper bluffs
　But never (no!) succumbs.

"More water!" "Stoke the firebox well!"
　The engineer's sharp shout…
Now hear the crystal clang of bell,
　As we are moving out.

Across the trestle, tunnel through,
　Along the precipice,
We feel again what once they knew:
　The greatest trip there is.

GLIDER FLIGHT

Our hearts jumpstarted
When the tiny tow-plane's
Engine left our silent craft
To soar upon the air only,
Circled by eagle and hawk
Gliding, too, on currents—
Defeating logic yet airborne.
We were human kites aloft,
Learning to trust the whims
Of an unpredictable element.
Some, perhaps, would call it
Faith.

ANOTHER PLACE, ANOTHER TIME
Juneau, Southeast Alaska

Down by the piers, the ships pull in to dock,
Gulls circling, searching, swoop with haunting cry—
And time means tide, not told by any clock,
But by the phases of the opal moon.

The queenly cruise ships, graceful, white as swans,
And sailing ships, must tuck and fold their wings
As sunset turns the channel to deep bronze,
And quiet fogs the harbor for the night.

Before first sun, the great swan-ships are gone,
Changed to toy boats on far horizon's line,
And tiny tugboats pull big barges on
Down toward Seattle, where they load again.

And meanwhile, trawlers bring in their first catch—
Are greeted raucously by gulls once more;
The city's picnic-basket is the hatch:
Ten thousand meals are made of this cargo.

The land and water meld, down by the piers,
The waterfront a mix of rush and noise,
And never quite what it sometimes appears:
Tall tales from travelers; gossip from the gulls.

SEVENTEENTH CENTURY SONNET

The most mysterious of gifts is love:
If you give yours, and find it not returned,
Does that not then your purest motive prove?
A gift begrudged is only to be spurned!
Yet if your love be big enough to share,
Divide it and it doubles: two for one,
And swiftly will a broken heart repair,
No blessing kinder than love's benison.
Consider how it grows from the first seed,
Entwining vines of love to circle wide,
With fruit enough to nourish every need—
Where love is planted, fear cannot abide.
So would I ask, so long as I shall live,
For love enough for me, and love to give.

PARK PICTURE IN BLACK AND WHITE

Like etchings on the sky, the trees stand stark,
No leaves unfurled as banners in the wind
To herald the approach of warmth and Spring.
Still snowfields slow the joggers as they run;
Ice islands make small mirrors of the lake.
Yet Winter is not so invincible,
For we see through its fortress opening chinks
Of hope, as when a bravely soaring kite
Takes off, and tugs our hearts aloft with it.
And, look: the ducks are back! Too soon, of course,
Those feathered optimists predict a thaw;
Yet who knows but (this time) they may be right?
The creatures without clocks or calendars
May harbor more of wisdom than we know
And sap wells up within the leaf-lorn trees,
Yes, even while black branches like harpstrings
Stir distant music on a stage of snow.

Island Girl, to City Boy

Because we're parting and the summer's done,
What's left to swear our faithfulness upon?
A summer kind of love it was, this one.

Perhaps so gilded by the shimmering sun,
We never noticed how easily it was won—
But we must part because the summer's done.

As delicate as spider silk finespun
Our little season's romance was begun—
A summer kind of love it was, this one.

Though most who watched us thought it all in fun.
Truth was, I loved you more than anyone—
But you must leave because the summer's done.

I must not let my smile become undone;
You must not know how hard it is to run
From arms that held a summer's love—this one.

I will not bear regret, for I have none;
What better than a season in the sun?
Though we are parting and the summer's done,
It was a youthful fantasy of love, this one.

THE BARDS OF AUTUMN

If in our youth we always wished for Spring,
To see May flowers into arbors formed
To hear the birds' sweet-voiced remembering;
To touch safe harbor when the seas have stormed,
Then must we grow, mature, and graduate
From universities of life well-taught;
Succeed, unwillingly, to this estate:
We may not, by mid-life, find what we sought.
To recognize our limitations' bounds
Becomes a measure of our growth so far.
If we are luckier still, a cheer resounds
As one of us becomes a shooting star.
So may at last the bards of Autumn sing,
Forgetting nought; remembering everything!

AT THE SYMPHONY

Thread golden notes from brass, and silver harp
With rainbow chords, a blend of artistry;
The maestro's baton is a needle, sharp
And sure, to stitch a magic tapestry.
For color, add the bold contrabassoon,
And mellowed pastels from the violins.
The cello adds a luster all its own,
And, suddenly, the fabric's weave begins!
The pattern is perceived: two unicorns
Stand white against the backdrop of the woods;
An antlered deer peers out among the horns,
As fantasies drawn from our own childhoods.

Where does the music go when we have left?
Our memories are sturdy, firmly weft.

THE CRACKS IN THE GLAZE
This pitcher, made from earth,
> yet mirrors sky,
that crystalline, pure blue of
> wind-washed air.
Its surface bears a maze of tiny cracks,
A labyrinth of lines etched in the glaze.
It is a little history of life—
for here it was set down too hard, and
> there
it suffered from a surfeit of such use
one wonders how it could be filled again
and pour as freely as it did before
the limitless libations it has known.
To celebrate;
> to slake the thirst;
> to ease
more sombre celebrations to their ends...
At last to sit upon the middle shelf
regarded reverentially for worth
it did not have
> when it was
> shining new.

EVENSONG

Let the little sounds that beat all day like whirring
  wings against the air —
Their gentleness no protest to the shrieking noise:
Montage of traffic, factory whistles, all discordant,
  strident blare —
Let the muted sweetness of them now be given a belated
  voice.
And let all ears accustomed to the point of self-inflicted
  deafness, due
Anything that shrieks, let them (oh, most of all!) be
  reached by something new.

FAMILY REUNION

Long picnic tables, silvery as barnwood, fill
the grape arbor,
like ships in a harbor;
a reunion regatta.

They're freighted down with such a Summerful
cargo of primary-
color foods, culinary
fugue and toccata...

    such medleys of fruits and cheese and spices,
    such melodies of color, grape to peach!
    the grandmothers, the mothers, hope it suffices,
    leaves every celebrant too sated, far, for speech.

"Don't you TOUCH that!" rings out with authority;
a small hand creeps
back from cornucopia heaps
of food to table's thin edge.

One table alone holds a dozen kinds of pastry;
oozing with juice
of summer's fruits;
small hand sneaks a slim wedge.

babies tumble like a litter of round kittens
near the feet of their
preoccupied mothers,
make exploratory mews.

"Now tell about the table where the salad glistens."
Sprigged with parsley,

dressed with oil, shiny
in the green cool.

Some sparkle with ripe fruit in gelatines;
some are shaped, are ringed or welled or
mounded;
some return to where the families begin;
their origins are sure to be expounded.

Under a net canopy, crowned with pineapple rings,
reigns the handsomest ham,
reason enough for some aunt's fame;
it's fragrant with rehydrated love.

The round and rosy ladies of three motherings
frankly share their best,
wanting all the rest
to taste their life, and find it good.

Remember, remember, say sisters to each
other,
remember, remember, calls cousin to cousin.
Remarks one favorite aunt, "You look just like
your
mother!"
We smile in concord: "That's what we've
BECOME."

LULLABY

Sleep. For while I love you
Nothing of the earth shall harm you,
Nothing of the day or of the night.

In the glare of the sun, my hand
Will shield your eyes until it burns,
And then it will not fall. Sleep.

In the lash of the storm, my back
Will cut the cold until it dies,
And then it will not bend. Sleep.

Sleep. But, while I love you,
Nothing of the earth shall have you;
Nothing else will ever set you free.

BIRD CALLS

The rocks are ribs; the ridges form
The spine, to make a mountain live:
And trees that bend before a storm
Seem breathing entities that thrive
On earth and water, air and fire—
Anatomy is like this land:
The structure is the skeleton
Which one must fully understand
As did the artist Audubon,
Who brought us news about the birds,
Who feathered their frail bones for flight,
Who favored flocks instead of herds;
Who saw eternity alight
In guise of pure white winged dove,
The first from Noah's Ark to bring
A message of forgiving love.
Birds are the voices; they can sing
In language always understood.
Birds are the hope, on winged thrust
Of what we might be, if we could —
Or what we can be, if we must.
What other creatures show the way,
Inscribed in arcs across the sky?
Let him who thinks he stands, they say,
Be wary lest he fall awry.
Such little sermons on the wing
Are lost on those who cannot sing.

HOPPER'S HOUSES

"The answer is on the canvas!"
Edward Hopper to those who asked, "What does it mean?"

Cape Cod Morning. The tawny-haired woman
looks anxiously out her front window
assessing the strength of early-day sun:
will it last long enough to dry her weekly wash?
Will the salty air a chance gust blows there
Make pillowcases billow like a small boat's sails?
If sun burns off fog, can she still hear the foghorns?
She loves the foghorns; they seek something, as she does.

Cape Cod Afternoon. Half in light, half in shadow,
at four o'clock the house shows a closed door;
windows a blank stare with no figure behind them;
even the dog is unseen, napping perhaps
in some cool, mysterious place his humans
would not think to look so cannot disturb him.
Soon the kitchen will send out succulent signals
that dinner is in the works—the dog will return.
Cape Cod Evening. Behind the house, the woods
form a dusky blue shade. Late afterglow strikes
the front of the house, turning the white paint
shrill as a gull's cry. It is after dinner now;

the tawny-haired woman has donned a fresh blue dress
for her man's homecoming. He has shed city clothes
to play with his pet Collie whose coat is a painterly
echo of the woman's hair—no accident, you may be sure.
But the dog's focus is drawn away by a bird's cry—
not one of the beings in the scene relates to another.

Hopper's houses are made of more than wood and stone;
Sometimes they wear human guise, or animal—
But always and ever they are alone.

DUSK: FROM A HILL

Now, only
one thin slice
of all the loaf
that was this day
remains.

It must be
savored,
every crumb,
so thoughtfully

that it will be
remembered when
tomorrow's scales
shall weigh

too short:
It is our
present
comfort and
our future prayer.

HOT PINK

More red flowers bloom there
than I have ever known—
blood-flowers, some of them.
Heat rises in wavy spirals
from pitted flagstones,
burnished pink by rain
falling suddenly
as if a hand had let drop
a curtain of bright beads.
A little mangey cur laps
at an irridescent puddle
in a frenzy before it evaporates
in this shimmering air,
just as the painter
at his easel across the way
frantically dabs and scrubs
from canvas to palette
and back again
before it gets away from him.

Blossoms drop; new red blooms.

DISTANCES

Because I do not know,
Because I do not want to know
How far it is from where I am
To where you are,

I play myself a game,
A small, evasive kind of game,
The rules are mine — always the same:
How far to where you are?

Just hours by air
(And hundreds of nonexistent dollars)
But I could gather all my garden's flowers
And bring them to you, fresh as dawn
If I got on an East-bound plane,
If life would play my game.
Because I do not know,
Because I do not care to know
How far it is from where I am
To where you are,
The phone springs to my feckless hand;
I dial you, feeling reckless, and
Place the desk clock on its face,
Because I do not care to see
How many minutes it may pace
Of talk on rented wires,
Outflow from you and me.

Because I do not know,
Because I do not need to know
How far it is from where I am
To where you are...
It is as long as a deep sigh.

PROTECTIVE ARMOR

Shimmer
　Shiver
　　Glitter
　　　Gleam…

Frail armature,
Shoulderblades like
Sparrow wings,
Dressed in satin
Of a silver sheen,
　　　Clothes the singer
At the last show
On Saturday night
Must have borrowed.
Only her song tells
It true: Her heart
Wears a ragged coat,
No proof against the cold.

A SHOPPING-MALL-SHAPED POEM

I only went there for a spool of thread,
A means to mend my life,
To make my self presentable again.
But then
I was assaulted on all sides
By new appeals:
"TO MAKE YOU THINNER! NOW! THE SPA!
"TO MAKE YOU UNFORGETTABLE —
"CASBAH, THE NEW COLOGNE!
"TO MAKE YOU OVER—" "TO MAKE YOU... "
As if, perhaps, I had
Not yet been born?
The jeweler's window dazzled,
The record shop played antidotes
To the bland music
Permeating the arcade,
Sarabandes of sweetness
As cloying as incense.
Aromas of indulgences
As yet untapped —
Did I want popcorn

In a dozen tastes?
Or else a double-chocolate cone?
A dozen roses, plastic-wrapped
And drooping on their stems
Before they even left the shop?
No, none of these,
Together or alone,
Would be my choice,
    If choose I could!
I came out to the brightness,
Into the sun again,
Clutching just one small paper bag,
Victorious over all temptations.
    I only went there, as I said,
    To buy a spool of thread.

RAISED HOPES

Let's fly a skyfull of all kinds of kites—
The kind a boy can make, himself, from scraps,
That wags a tail of rags to reach new heights.
Red box-kites tugging hearts aloft, perhaps,
And Japanese kites, shaped like silver fish...
And kites that educate—a dinosaur!
So self-important, filling no child's wish,
Unlike that kite which struggles free and soars
And leaves its owner only: broken string,
Or so, at any rate, it sadly seems...
The rogue kite makes a small boy's heart to sing,
Its journey all his own most secret dreams.

Look now! Confetti swirls of color sweep
The sky, and we have memories to keep.

TRAVELOG: COUNTRY CALLED TIME

If tutored by the ticking tongues of clocks
Or coached by sibilant calendar leaves
To nudge us from a fussy prompter's box,
We might well learn the language; but reprieves
For impulses—blithe byways—are unknown.
One must, I think, abjure the traveler's vice:
To see and smell and taste the texture here,
And never read the guidebook over twice,
Nor let familiar songs seduce the ear,
Nor any wish for dalliance ever own.

The arbitrary architecture here
Is structured elements with terraces—
Baroque in the beginning, now austere:
The curled Corinthian embarrasses;
Compatible is Doric's cubic square,
But old Ionic's scroll's to dust consigned.
So let the traveler's wayward foot beware
What he with serendipity might find.
A fine place for a visit—rankling rare—
It's only living there I cannot bear.

CRUNCH

"Your future lies in the fate of this cookie." — *Message from a Chinese fortune cookie*

Discovering this dire pronouncement,
Fragilely sheathed in pastry crescent,
I naturally took all precautions:
Wrapped the harbinger in oceans
Of cotton from blue box with red cross,
Guarding against the sudden loss
Of rowdy health and garrulous speech
Wanting no misfortune to teach
What might be learned from sharp adversity
(Dropping out of <u>that</u> University),
And one day woke to a grey and grim sky,
Took my bearings, heaved a great sigh,
Acknowledging here it was at last:
Not to be missed, the final bombast...
Please, don't wait up—I may be <u>very</u> late;
I am going out to find my fate.

Far off, the distant cannon rumbles;
Someone was hungry; the cookie crumbles.

OLD PAWN BRACELET

It has that soft patina of old silver,
Much prized, much polished, worn
Sunrise to sunset, work to dancing,
Never taken off until a leaden day
Of too much hunger and no money.

You can see: the wrist that wore it
Had once been young and rounded,
But thinned by too many hard years;
There are faint lines in the silver
From bending it smaller and smaller.

Who was she, the old Zuni woman?
The rightful owner of this silver prize,
Her spirit still so strong I even hesitate
To pay the price and claim it for my own.
Somewhere, she knows it is hers, always.

CAPITOL HILL ON A SUNNY MORNING

The mortar here is promises, grey stone
And marble, bound by words that echo still
Within these chambers, high upon a hill.
No man can tread these corridors alone.
Proud banners flying, flank the golden dome,
And tell of history, resolved and writ,
Immutable as distant stars are lit,
Unchanging as the words of ancient tomes.
Brave colors! Raised at sunrise every day,
They furl and unfurl with the changing breeze,
And guide the Ship of State on stormy seas.
Magnificent, heart-stirring, they allay
Old fears and new. Their promises are kept:
The heritage of men who long have slept.

GHOST TOWN NEAR RED MOUNTAIN

Dust devils.
Trust me:
That's just
stray winds
that mime
riderless
horses' hooves
on old Main Street.

Isn't it?

And only random winds
again that
fill the bellows
of the church
organ, playing
half-forgotten
hymns by rote.

Trust me.

For who could
pull the ragged rope
that makes the bell
of the old schoolhouse
ring out again,
so pure and clear
in this deserted
valley air?

Of course, we are alone!
(At least, I trust we are...)

SEVEN A.M.
My darling, from the deep
Scuba-land of sleep
You seem regretfully to surface.
What trophy do you bear
Back to the deck-flat everyday?
You seem now fretfully
To speak
But words are still aqueous.
One hand clutches,
Other wards away
And none could say
If you protect
What you have
Or else reject
What you love,
But dare not keep.
There are wrecks down there, down deep,
Of dreams, your own and others' sleep.

"ALL THE PRETTY LITTLE HORSES"
Hush-a-bye, and don't you cry,
Go to sleepy, little baby —
When you awake, you shall have cake,
And all the pretty little horses… "

—from an Appalachian lullaby

They feel it first, the colts and ponies do,
The very essence of a Rocky Mountain Spring.
You see them shake their manes and sniff the air,
Their noses twitching with a glad remembering.
Their shaggy coats become more glossy now;
Perked ears take on alertness for a certain sound,
And, questioning, their eyes grow much too bright,
As, prancing their delight, they trot the pasture round.
Just at the meadow's edge, an old fruit tree
Still blossoms. Wind makes petals into pink snowfall,
This season which is both an end and start,
And oh! the pretty little horses love it all.

SONG OF THE ADOBE HOUSE

The women came to shape my bricks,
Their fingers quick and sure;
The children stirred my mud with sticks;
The sunlight baked me pure.

The men, they heaved the rafters high,
Their muscles straining hard:
My structure rose against the sky,
But in a barren yard.

The women made me pretty, then,
With flowers circling round,
But gently teased by all the men
Who raised me from the ground.

"What good are flowers here? They'll die!"
So scoffed the men, each one.
The women heard me, wistful, sigh,
And left nothing undone.

My window-eyes look out upon
An ancient mountain-range,
Like me, earth-born in times agone,
Like me, and so not strange.
The women gave me eyes to see,
And flowers for my soul;
The men all worked in harmony,
Each certain of his role.

But more, to me, the children's songs,
As, happily, they played —
Each family, to me belongs…
And all of them have stayed.

BIOGRAPHY: THE NAVAJO

The purity of line
Is woven in the blankets:
    Colors of earth,
    Colors of sky.
The spirit there,
    In warp and weft,
And used therefore
    For living,
    For dying,
And all the needs between.
The blankets used
To make a shelter
    From strong sun;
    To wrap a baby:
    To warm an Old One;
    To make a bed
    Beneath the stars...
And, finally,
    A winding-sheet,
That the Great Spirit
    Recognize
This was one who trod
His ways... and did it well.

THE WIND-GARDENER

A wild flower is a weed become a friend,
The way one might describe, say, Queen Anne's Lace:
From wind-blown seeds come nosegays for the heart.
There's Indian Paintbrush, colors splashed across
A valley vista, there for all who dare
To climb that high to see, a live landscape.
There's Columbine, five petals porcelain-thin,
Translucent cup, transcendent bravery
Withstanding all the weather's whims and winds.
The sagebrush blooms and scents the arid air
With pungence all its own: desert perfume.
Above the timberline, a tiny star
Of white, as pure as hope, conquers the odds
Against it, digs in, clings to a short life
If that's what the gods send—who knows which way
The wind will blow next time, how far away?

LOVE IN A LOAF OF FRESH–BAKED BREAD

The scent of cinnamon's magnetic force,
The yeastiness of baking bread unmatched
For pure allure: all steps lead to the source
On homecoming, as soon as door's unlatched.
The kitchen is a gathering-place for love,
Each act nurturing a testament.
A random reach in cookie jar will prove
Your favorites are there, and circumvent
All notions of your lack of self-esteem.
The one who loves you best baked all of these:
To show your world less harsh than it might seem;
To find warmth there, and comfort, and heartsease.

Is love life's leaven, causing it to rise?
Do you doubt what you see with your own eyes?

"S"

The road to Durango
Curves and uncoils
Glossily, snakelike,
Traffic hissing by
Like endless "S"'s on
The precipice's edge.
A vast yet virgin valley
Lies in wait below,
A soft, seductive vista
Luring the eye's focus
From the hypnotic hiss.
It takes only a second
To immerse oneself in this
Destructive spell, element.
A sensuous seizure seems
To sing "Serenity Forever."

JOHN DONNE AT DAWN
Upon a country road in Oregon,
Two jubilant joggers meet in chill-gray dawn:
The fog enwraps them like their hooded shirts;
Beneath their urgent feet, sprayed water spurts.

Adidas pounding out a metric beat,
Iambic rhythms rise and fall, repeat.
Obscured by mist, the ghost of old John Donne
Counts cadence as they run, in unison:

"Go and catch a falling star! ... "
Tell me where all past years are!"

Still chasing stars in 1631,
The brightest in the firmament was Donne.
A star fell, surely, when his own light dimmed.
Three centuries are gone, his lines still hymned
By this unlikely pair with few past years,
The sounding of their feet applauds, reveres.

These two are met upon a winding road,
And none can say what may their future bode.

"Must to thy motions lovers' seasons run?"
Asked John Donne when he saw the rising
sun.

I ask John Donne, in Heaven's high estate,
To plead for these two, running, a kind fate:
May roads be ever smooth beneath their feet,
And hills crest gently, as their runs complete.

TRAIL RIDGE VISTA

There are no softly-rounded edges:
This country asks no quarter, and gives none.
At timberline, the soil's unfriendly;
There's none to spare for Nature's gardening—
And yet you'll see the frailest flowers
Abloom wherever last year's seeds have blown.
Bare roots cling to the cloven rocks, here,
And trees grow one side only in this wind.
Still, they endure: they bend; submit; bow —
They green the grey, unyielding stone… and stay.

NATURE IN TOOTH AND CLAW

The small and skittery white cat nextdoor
who looks as demure as Emily Dickinson,
who flees when my hand reaches for a pat,
stalks a hapless, even smaller creature:
a pinkeared fieldmouse, rapid heartbeat
so agitated it threatens to burst, terrified,
from the sweet downiness of its chest.
Cat is (probably) not thinking terrorism,
just playing, batting this furry little ball
from one paw to the other, claws sheathed
until instinct makes her mindless, the word,
mercy, missing from the lexicon of cats!

LONE TREE AT TIMBERLINE
They still come back,
The woodchucks and the birds;
They brave fierce winds
To visit me again,
Though there is nothing left
For them to eat.
They chatter and they chirp
As cheerfully
As if a forest feast
Awaited them,
As it did, far below...
And long ago.
The forest may still yield
Some forage there,
But up here, where the earth
Can scarce conceal
My old, tenacious roots,
And I am bent
In labyrinthine lines,
A silhouette
Of question marks that ask:
How long have I?
How long before the wind
Claims all my soil,
And all my sap, my life? ...
The edelweiss,
That little plant of hope,
Goes on... and on.

A Keen-Eyed View

(Sam Keen to a rock "Damn it! You tripped me!" —from To: A Dancing God)

We are accustomed to their silence;
<u>The immutable silence of stones,</u>
Is how we think.
    But if you heard
Some troll-like voice cry, "Ouch!
You kicked me!" would you not bend
A little closer, ear to ground?

If you were thinking of The Wall,
That wall of stones you always meant
To build someday to keep life
And the raucous world it's lived in
At a safe distance, perhaps, yet
Were enchanted by this rock's colors,
Might you not haul it homeward?

And <u>then,</u> if you had progressed beyond
Annoyance and utility to admiration;
If you had dared to let in for once
The possibility that all nature
Does not conspire to trip you up—
Is there a chance that you might find
And know your place?
    Solid, as they say,
    As a rock?

THE WOUND AND THE KNIFE

"You cut me!" said the wound, gaping.
Sorry, I felt nothing at all, said the knife.

"I tasted blood," said the mouth.
"I had to suck the wound. Awful."
I've never tasted blood, said the knife.

"I saw it; sticky red," said the eyes.
"It spurted, it formed pools. Scary."
Never been scared, said the knife.

"I hurt; don't you care?" said the wound.
The business of knives is merely cutting,
Not caring what they cut, said the knife.

"But YOU did it!" accused the wound.
No more than I would slice a peach,
Or slit open a letter, said the knife.

I am only a tool, said the knife.
You will have to look elsewhere
To fix your blame, said the knife.

"I need help now!" screamed the wound.
"I can be mended to meet tomorrow."
"Good luck," said the knife.
There are a lot of knives out there… just waiting.

BIRTHDAY BLESSING

We change, the wily scientists avow,
Once every seven years —
So you begin another life from now;
Adventure reappears
On far horizons never viewed before.
How do you read the sky,
As wayfarer and traveler once more?
What, with your artist's eye,
Do you perceive, interpret, then evaluate?
You rush toward destiny!
We wish you only a rewarding fate:
A Mozart symphony,
A Summer sky without a darkening cloud,
a picnic in the park,
A friend to share what you dare say aloud!
A candle for the dark.

TERROR FOR BREAKFAST

Propping the pristine paper against a pitcher
I see the front page photo, in mid-winter grey
and grainy but for the swath of police tape
spewing its yellow scream: DANGERDANGER
where terrible acts broke midnight silence
only eight hours before.
There is a depression
in the white where some unlucky one, fallen,
made a live snow-angel, hands outstretched
forming wings, while pleading for his life.
So: no need for the crime-scene chalk outline
marking where the latest bullet felled a boy
not even yet a man.
My snug small house is no fortress, its walls
not impregnable, its silvery ribbons of security
wired to alarms no guarantees.
On such a day as this
I wrap myself in mittens and muffler, not even
looking at thermometers.
It suddenly seems unbearably cold out there.

Nuns at the Circus

They flutter like a flock of bluebirds here,
Heads coiffed in Heaven's color. But how young
They look! Bright-faced as their small charges are,
These sparrow-children of the poor, rich now:
No poverty within the circus rings.
It's magic! Glories feed their hungry eyes.
The elephants bear howdahs bright with jewels,
And sequinned acrobats, all sparkle, shine,
Leave paths like diamonds tracing through the air,
The nuns conducting symphonies of joy:
The chirps and giggles buoyantly ring out
And there's a chorus of applause for all:
The dazzling creatures on the highest wire;
The sparrows and the bluebirds down below.

Notes on a River called Time

Midstream, this suddenly narrowed river,
Here only a little, dappled brook,
Surprisingly seems not to go on forever,
Over glistening shoals of golden sand
As when we were ridiculously young.
Enter an endless perspective:
We are among sunlit shadows, bright and dark,
And here a smooth pool invites our reflective
—Not vain, but thoughtful—look.
Do we now ever gratefully recall
A certain, green-gold summer's day?
Do we remember the strength and pull
Of one who swam these waters far better
Than we thought we could, urging us on and on?
Midstream is a time for catching breath
And taking stock, and much, much less of talk.
Let's take <u>one</u> more dive! Say, "Yes" —it's fun.
Water carries voices down the stream, calling us Home.
You'd better hurry, though—it's getting late.

ART NOUVEAU DREAMS

The interior landscape of mind dreaming
is purest Art Nouveau, color and pattern
astonishing in mutability.

I ache with nostalgia, a longing for a time
I never knew, when Beardsley and McCay,
Parrish and Erté,

made the fevered fabric of their canvases
as lush as Gauguin's jungles, bright as those
wheatfields of Van Gogh.

I wake from Art Nouveau to cityscapes
of concrete canyons, misted grey with fog,
where I must stay... by day.

A Visit with my Aunt

Sing me a song of faraway lands;
Tell me of bygone times!
Let me hold history here in my hands;
Spin me a yarn that limns
Each generation's telling anew
What you remember now:
Tales your own teachers <u>re</u>told to you,
Reaching for "WHY?" and "HOW?"
When did my people set out to roam?
Why did they settle here?
How did they know when they had come home?
What did they pioneer?
Proud as I am to hear of their deeds
(Braver, by far, than mine),
Each is a candle, lit for my needs,
Hallowed by history's shrine.

No Trumpets

I thought there would be trumpets when we met,
And cymbals crashing like a thunderstorm
When we, at long last, found each other's lips.

I wondered at the time if Cupid had
Miscued us both. There we were, caught by rain,
Entranced too deep for seeking shelter yet,
Warmed by our own small inner fire, amazed
At how compelling kisses are, when right.

Too soon, we had to go back to our friends,
Whose lamplit windows we could see from where
We were — but suddenly too shy to share.

You took your own coat off, wet though it was,
And tented it above our heedless heads.
We laughed; it was belated chivalry,
But still—I did not miss the trumpets then
And never have, in all the years between.

X-Ray: The Interior Landscape

Here works the Ansel Adams of the bones.
He searches out the shadows of one's self
For truth: where hides the fracture, where the cells
Are merged into a mass of mystery.
Your bones and ligaments and tendons bared,
The smallest fissure shown as an abyss:
The plates remind of Adams' classic shot,
The Moon Above Yosemite, its planes of rock,
Of peaks and valleys almost skeletal.

Yet, having marveled, peering at the plates,
This patient sighs, the picture incomplete,
Deluded by a quest: to seek her soul.

THE UNDERSIDE OF STONES

This stone came from Oregon's coast;
A small Henry Moore sculpture it is,
Hole like a window through which to see
A different world. Two smaller stones
Cling to the hollow, having clung
Through tides both ebb and flow,
Their bottoms serrated like teeth.

If you have ever walked upon a beach
Along the coast of Oregon, you know
Why this tenaciousness. No soft sand
Takes your footprint; it is one stone
After another, ranging from pebbles
To boulders—take care walking there.

Now, this one beckoned from a posted
Falling Rock Zone—serendipitous because
Its mica brightness beaconed out
From an otherwise indistinguishable
Heap. That it survived the rockfall
Is a wonderment. It flakes, you see,
Unlike the hardier specimens, built up
From strata, visible layers of time.
But how can one resist it? It shines

So in the sunlight, and it fits just
Right into a jeans pocket to take home.
Set in the side garden, it need know
No more harsh traveling, and can endure.
Finally, my favorite stone. You see
This fish, its bony shape imprinted
Like a petroglyph? It tells us in
A literal translation that once,
Eons ago, where we stand was ocean,
Or glacier melt, or a great flood...
The underside is smooth as an egg,
Another sign that water has washed it.
I look at this fish fossil and think
How children form snow-angels,
Making their bid for immortality
(When this you see, remember me).

But sun melts angels made of snow,
And stone let fall can shatter history.

NOTES ON A RAINY NIGHT IN SPRING

What matters is: not lightning, thunder, or
That hovering cloud above the distant hills—
What matters is, I think, the scent of rain
When everything so longs to bloom anew.

When, finally, the rain comes, curtain-like,
A new show' s staged—it' s almost magical.
The stage directions read: "Go for a stroll."

No better time to walk on country lanes,
Where lilac fragrance meets the smell of loam
Made sharper by the touch of Springtime rain.

Our memories are filled with rainy walks,
Roads taken for discoveries of love,
Or ways to ward off love's acute despair.

On city streets, reflections neon-bright
May shimmer on wet pavements as you walk,
And street musicians syncopate the night;
A bitter blues goes well with tears of rain.

Jane Davis Carpenter

TIME FROZEN: FAMILY ALBUM
Their image shimmering on the air,
Together, in a too-big chair,
My daughter and a sleepy cat
Still occupy the place they sat,
To catch the Winter's lemon sun
When she was five, and he was one.
They waited somnolent, the two,
For someone passing, someone who
Had hugs to spare, or pats for cats.
Since then, of course, their thermostats
Predict a harsher weather now!
They ask for what life will allow.

TROUT HANGOUT
(The Frying Pan River Near Basalt)

Under the wands of the green willow tree,
The river narrows here to a calm stream;
Tamed enough to tempt fishers of trout,
Who endure the water's all but frozen flow
Over expensively booted feet now numbed.
The trout, though, thrive in such a chill,
Their silvery skins like coats of mail
Protecting that sweet, delicate flesh beneath.

Solitude and silence are other reasons
To wait with patience for revealing splash.
Ah, but splash reveals danger, too,
To wilier trout who plunge emerald depths
To bottom, pretending to be river stones
Of little interest to a greedy fisherman.
Where else, it might be fair to ask,
Can a man give the illusion of occupation
While doing absolutely nothing but waiting?

You could say: both creatures abide
In their truest element. I would.

Ducks on Lollipop Lake

*Garland Park is one of the prettiest 'pocket parks' in
the city; next to an elementary school in location, and
featuring a small, round pond. The pond, because of the
children who flock around it daily, is called Lollipop Lake.
This poem was written in November, and is a Thanks-Giving poem.*

The little lake is rimmed with rime,
Yet in its deepest center, ripples flow.
There, warmth's retained, from endless summer days;
The ducks remember summer, so they go—
Aglide, as graceful as swan-sisters now—sail!
As ballerinas waddle when they walk,
When that mysterious message comes to flock
And fly to kinder climates when the turn
Of treacherous weather comes! They catch the heart
With their well-ordered numbers taking flight.
Of this same universe, we are a part,
For all that we walk awkwardly at times,
In elements against our natural bent,
And flutter helplessly when we are lost,
And wonder if our faith is fraudulent.
When we know cold, we can remember warm;
Envised by pain, release is pleasure pure;
When we are hungry, we are somehow fed,
For all else passes; yet will God endure.

STILL LIFE
The pearly sheen of fruit set on the windowsill,
Round cheek of apple; curve of pear, turned toward the
   sun,
Reminds of old Dutch paintings.
Look! How the dust-motes dance in that bright shaft;
See! How the curtains billow softly in the breeze;
Listen! To the birdsong filtered through the hush of sleepy
   noon.

All this is happening upon a certain Summer's day,
The one that just precedes the Fall's first frost—
The one that, yearly, takes us by surprise.
Unfairly, we, who should remember other Autumns, fail:
The natural progression find once more too quick.

Our consolation is:
THIS is the moment when that fruit
Is ripe and ready.
We have watched, and seen, and listened.

Are we ready now to taste?

THE COLOR OF HOPE

Hope's color should, they say, stay ever green,
When all the landscape's etched in graven white
And ice has stilled what late was splashing stream.
Earth's memory's engraved alike, and wise
In ways of Nature's order and Her plan,
To give the burgeoning and bloom a rest—
She draws a silver curtain with Her hand!
But still our eyes and hearts need <u>hope</u>; attest
To the indomitable spirit's faith. . .
In searching out the green of spruce and pine,
The canopies of trees whose shelters make
A feeding-place for birds and squirrels to dine:
Beneath those spreading boughs are cones and seeds;
Are stored the souvenirs of Summer's reign,
And every winter sojourner who feeds
Enriches furred-or-feathered self again,
While brightening the otherwise gray scene.
For these small creatures, let us now give thanks,
They show us what, to us, is barren plain—
Explored, becomes a phalanx of hope's flanks.

BRAIDING BETSY'S HAIR

Present, past and future here
Twine themselves as one—
Brushing, braiding Betsy's hair
In the morning sun.
This is magic time for us,
Braiding close our lives:
As I stroke with rhythmic brush,
Time long gone revives
And renews our bond once more:
Child who sits and hears;
Mother needing to explore
Past and future years.

MADAME GREETS HER NEW CLASS

How many has the mirror shimmered back
Across the years, caught in its silver view?
The seasons in Madame's own almanac
Are marked by "Swan" and "Nutcracker" anew;
Small duckling to be transformed into swan,
And tomboy leaps, to fairy tour jetés,
The air an element to glide upon.
Some will not know the magic, all their days,
But, now and then, a foot will arch just so—
A hand will reach for that elusive rose;
Together, notes and dancer seem to flow.
For this, she strikes her most majestic pose,
And motes of dust in sunlight shafts unseen,
The little ones are members of her court—
And she is once again the reigning queen.
From out the past, new dreams come to transport.

POLAROID INSTANT

On a blue-domed, late-summer day,
We are being sea-creatures, beached
By green-glass, crashing waves.

Our daughter, sea-nymph for now,
Is brushing sand and salt
From out her long, sun-streaked hair,
Sand- and salt-covered silken strata.

Her father, stealthily, picks up camera
To capture the naiad no net can catch.
In that Polaroid instant, I cast back
My net of memory and superimpose another
Image over hers: myself at 14, and it matches!

Somewhere, under this slim, well-oiled machine
Of a well-preserved woman there remains a girl.
I announce recklessly to our fetching nymph,
Who knows no need of subterfuge or subtleties,
"I'll race you down to the ice-cream stand!"

Pray for me, all you baskers in the sun,
All you watchers of the sea;
I need this tiny victory.

ALL I WANTED WAS A DOLL
After a painting by Josef Head

None too willing
is she to give
her flower-stalk waist to the making
of a child; nor almond-tipped hands
to dig in dirt, make clean the house,
bake the loaf for her love's waking:
none too willing
is she to live.

It is enough to be,
she tells the green bird
tied to a shortening leash;
she speaks her futile word
me, her only guarantee
on this fragile day
in an orange-sunned May
of perpetually rosy flesh,
always-shining hair
upon a canvas square.

REFLECTIONS IN A MIRROR OF THE PAST
Long after smudges of small fingerprints
have all been polished out of existence,
and toys mysteriously strewn all over
the just-cleaned, party-perfect house,
and wilting bouquets of prize flowers
with snapped-off stems were left for you,
and cakes for the church bake sale
were nibbled at, leaving telltale crumbs —
you look around your quiet, tidy house
and wish with all your heart to have
such sweet disorder restored to you again.

FEATHERS FROM STONE
Gary Eagle Plume Sculpts a Warrior Chieftain

Inside the rock
Inside the roughness
Waits the sleek skin
Polished and proud
Over sharp cheekbones
Over taut throat muscles
Stretched over bow-arm

This I will find
For I know it is there
Tap-tap the echo
Of my seeking chisel
Sharp like the drumbeat
Louder and louder
-Closer and closer

The drums for war
A giant's heartbeat
An angry giant heedless
Of peace-pipe and prayers
My brother in rock
Must wear warrior guise
Trophy feathers in hair

Now will you ask me:
Make feathers from stone?
How almost impossible!
You will wonder aloud.
Not as hard, I swear
As showing his eyes sad
As only war makes them.

REMEMBERING EMILY
Emily Dickinson, 1830–1886

The quiet courtyard still
Recalls the Belle of Amherst well,
And ivy greening her small bed
May weave a wreath around her head.

The songs of lark and mockingbird
Might be the sounds she once heard
A hundred years ago and more,
Reprising like a sweet encore.

On Sundays long ago, she strolled
These grassy pathways here and told
Her spirit-visions to no one,
As silent as a cloistered nun.

Demure she was, dressed all in white,
An unimposing figure, slight
As any cygnet's quill she penned
Her lines with, even to the end.

At dusk, when evening shadows fall,
The bell for Vespers sounds its call.
Thus it may happen; some shall see
The wraith of 1883.

As gauzy as sheer-winged moth
A specter not of flesh and cloth,
But spirit, rises from her rest
Miss Dickinson to manifest.

THE LAMP-LIT WINDOWS

Seen from a passing train,
a hundred miles since tree
or creature or shabby shack
broke flat horizon line
suddenly a wayside cabin
becomes an architecture
for the mind's imaginings.

Warm and welcoming yellow
glow the windows at just-dusk,
the time of day the traveler
most longs for such a haven.

the train known as the Zephyr
races on, its own wheel-wind
bending prairie grasses low.

Encapsulated in the dining car,
a well-fed man sighs and pays
his check, longing for a place
and time her never knew…
except for that brief passing view.

Home, say the lamp-lit windows
to the heart of the romantic;
Come back, the train wheels whisper,
before becoming Clickety-clack.

BUSYBODY

The Navajo equivalent of "Busybody": "Someone who tells sheep which weed to eat"

Because the world is full of straying sheep
At least as far an Angus is aware
The border collie does not dare to sleep.

The valley floor is dense with heather, deep;
When trod upon, it scents the evening air—
Because the world is full of straying sheep.

Like some old vicar, now must Angus keep
His vigil, sensing peril somewhere;
The border collie does not dare to sleep.

Nearby, a wolf might chance to bide, to creep
From out his hidden mountain lair
Because the world is full of straying sheep.

But Angus watches while the lambkins leap
To save his flock from being Lobo's fare,
And keep them from the verdant mountain steep
Because the world is full of straying sheep.

SECRETS OF THE STONE
Her hands are small but able, scarred
from many a random slip of chisel,
many a gypsy chip of granite
seen too late to duck, perceived
as motes in sunlit shafts of studio light.
Her eyes are bright as polished lapis,
one brow convex as a circumflex,
arched in permanent surprise
(another chip struck, another time).

A dangerous place, this, where vast
and unforgiving stones resist the sculptor,
behaving like creatures from the wild
and she, their tamer. She tells them
truth, with every hammer blow she strikes:
she only wants to set their spirit free.
And if that spirit should take shape,
Some form not even she could hope for?
Then that is what she and the stone were
born for, and that the path
that led them to each other.

WATER RIGHTS

Like the last slice of watermelon,
Juicier than all the rest,
The last day of summer
Is savored, seeds and all!

The pool is open one last time,
So, like some sea-creature
With unseen fins,
I head back for one final plunge.

It's icy on my sun-warmed skin;
I am an instant mermaid in its chill,
Needing to move, and dive, and
Swish my imaginary, now-vestigial tail;
This is my element: my fire; my air.

But, as I dry upon the shore,
I realize again that summer
Is a sometime thing:
Three months allotted out of all the year
To take another view; to dream new dreams;
To plan for insubstantial sand-castles
There is no blueprint charting ways to make.

The dreams are part of summer's charm;
We eat of summer's fruits and sip her wine;
We wear light clothes, not armor to protect;
We think all things are possible,
And, possibly, they <u>are</u>.

I would not
    miss
      this
        last
          slice
            of
              watermelon
                  for
                    ANYTHING!

ITINERARY

Your smile that breaks so gently through your face,
Beginning in your eyes and traveling down
To curve your cheek more sweetly than before,
Enclose your mouth in deep parentheses,
And tilt your chin up quizzically, will reach
Its destination when it finds my heart.
This is a journey—though I know it well—
I never tire of charting yet again.

EPITAPH FOR A POET

This poet's epitaph is cut
In stone too massive for her, put
In place perhaps too soon. One shroud fits most,
But none for these sparse pearly bones.

They would exude a perfumed dust
Of days displaced, of short-time loans.

Inter her, rather, cryptically...
Wrap her in linen, like a nun—
Enfold her form elliptically
When her long fingers drop the pen.
Let her unwritten visions rise
To meet the sun, and gild the skies.

Colorado Boulevard Seen Late On a Rainy Saturday Night

The old "Chicago" bard
with his shock of hair
like cornsilk falling
over his Norse-blue eyes
and his shock of language
(don't forget how brave he
was or how tough he had to be)
nevertheless became soft
and sentimental about
—of all things!—
downtown traffic lights
seen from a homing plane.

He opined his City looked
like an emerald-and-ruby necklace
displayed on a black velvet
jeweler's cloth,
though one assumes
of Sandburg he knew little
of jeweler's showrooms
and cared even less about

ladies who wore their gems
instead of hocking them and
feeding a thousand of the poor.
Dear Carl, I need you at this
hopeless hour! My boulevard
wears cheap and gaudy finery
made out of vari-colored neon
and, what's more, I'm sure
     the gems
               are
                 only
                 glass.

SECOND SPRING

I would have gathered all my garden's flowers,
Still gemmed at dawn with little pearls of dew,
If they could possibly enhance the hours
Of lifetimes shared, of love-times spent with you—
But spent so recklessly! As if we could
Imagine all our wealth would last for years!
I tell you this: I always thought your good
Was strong enough to overcome my fears;
That there was nothing that could <u>not</u> be bought
With pledges and with tokens, I confess—
That we would find what we had always sought—
The odds a gambler would not even guess!

    This is the second Spring since you are gone,
    My garden flowers <u>still</u> as fresh as dawn.

TO MY DAUGHTER, ON HER 21ST BIRTHDAY

Of course, you were not meant to stay with us:
We raised you in the house, not unlike seedlings,
Knowing the time would come to transplant you,
And worry then about a killing frost,
Or worthless weeds that might get in your way;
Some, falsely pretty, like bindweed that chokes
While blooming with its own fair flowering;
Others, more recognizable as threats,
With jagged, knife-edged leaves, like dandelions.
The time has come: It's June, and seedlings grow.
The roots are strong and hardier; the plant
Now reaches to the sun, and spreads its leaves.

AT THE MENDENHALL GLACIER, ALASKA

Cathedrals made of glass might look like this,
With ancient ice turned blue as heaven's hue—
That being how the eye reads prism's gleam.
Low parapets wall off a deep abyss
To make more sure a climber's cleated shoe,
Aware that things are never what they seem.
If we could stand and stare, wide-eyed but still,
(The glacier is forever; only we
Remain ephemeral; it does not change)
We soon would see the glacier moves to fill
One part of Nature's vacuum, steadily,
And makes familiar what before was strange.

Colossus formed of crystals, one by one,
Bedazzles in the early Northern sun.

THE FRUITS OF FRIENDSHIP

Preserving a friendship
Is harvesting love,
A way of safekeeping
This practice may prove.

The grape left to ripen
Too long on the vine
Will never be savored
Unlike yours and mine

If, faithful, we follow
The lessons we learn;
We tend to our gardens
And reap what we earn.

The shine on an apple,
The bloom on a peach,
The roundness of melons,
The plum within reach;

The tartness of citrus,
A berry's sweet juice...
An aftertaste lingers
Of flavors profuse.

Preserving a friendship
Is harvesting love,
Like quilting, it's keeping
The past, lest it move.

THE CANDLES

Tradition wraps her like the warmest shawl,
As, eightfold, candles bless her quiet grace
Her children's faces ring her table now,
Some, come from distance of both time and place.

She is the keeper of these little flames,
The lights of Hanukkah and those of life;
She is the baker of the table's bread,
The household's queen, though but a poor man's wife.

Her husband sees her kissed by candlelight,
Each line upon her face a victory;
A happy miser, counting all their years
Like coins, and feeling rich as a grandee.

FLASHBACK, FAST FORWARD

We are in my Grandmother's sewing room
I trying to learn from her quick fingers
how to stitch together pieces of the past
for a new quilt, the design in her head
to be searched out. She is wrapped in
her favorite garment: a silk kimono of
that purple so rich and deep it rims the
sky at dusk; her favorite child, my father
gave her this… Whatever he gifts her with
becomes her favorite, so even I am included.

Grandmother's hand, shapely but well-used,
holds up a bright snippet of taffeta for me
to marvel at, a party dress once worn by a
long-dead aunt I never knew except for her
picture—she is wearing that wonderful dress
and a dimpled smile, delighted with herself.
She is eighteen forever, frozen in time
by the camera, and the scrap from her dress
is right here to see and touch, a leftover
life of its own to shine out from the quilt.

A whirr of calendar pages and my daughter,
a charming replica of that young aunt in the
sepia photograph, and delighted with her self,
is showing me her own design for a quilt,
so beautiful it looks like cathedral glass,
in which a rich, deep purple shimmers…
her tapered fingers (Grandmother's hands,
but new again) flick over the silken scraps,
pointing out woven memories, hers and mine.

HANDS

Hands folded beseech,
But they cannot hold;
Hands open can reach
And be blessed tenfold.

The pure art of loving is easy to learn—
Hold close with hands open and love will return.

Hands held like a cup
Can capture the rain
For thirst to drink up,
And be filled again.

So endless is love, why should we know greed?
To each shall be given according to need.

Hands touch and revive;
Tend babies; bake bread;
Make music of life,
Where love's always led.

OLD ECHOES

Around the festive board, old faces missed
Replace themselves with new ones: likeness-kissed—
The sweetness of a certain curve of cheek;
The tone of voice when one is heard to speak;
The grave regard of granite-colored eyes
Repeat the portraits on the wall; surprise
The senses with a spurt of memory
That answers every questing enquiry
(As potent as the scent of a pressed rose!).
How does a child reflect an aunt's repose,
Who never knew her mentor, long at rest,
But read her yellowed diary, frightened lest
The pages crumble in her smooth young hand?
A boy who knew not his ancestral land
Still bears the stamp of mountains and fjords;
The music's in his bones—the primal chords.
All that we have become, we owe the old
Who went before—their warmth would pierce the cold
Of this year's end and grey December day,
Where past has more than present words to say.

A Look at the Family Album

At twenty-two or so, my mother wore
The face of a rather knowing angel,
The faintest of lines beginning to appear,
Mouth's curve is half-seraphic,
Half-sophisticate;
Her tawny hair is back-lit soft to halo
That nearly-serene brow.
Her hands are folded like large lilies,
Thus telling little lies
About their capabilities.
This seeming seraph
Carried a canoe overland
And pitched a tent, and built a fire, and cooked,
And never once said she would rather be
Exploring concrete canyons in her own city.
She cleaned the fish my father caught,
Wrinkling her nose, but not
Refusing a gift from the stream,
Wrapped in sweet meadow-grass,
For breakfast…
And the day had just begun.

A Flower called Pain

It rives
from deep beneath
the dark, mysterious earth
awakened by the weather's moods.
What is this flower? <u>Some have called it Pain.</u>
Does it prefer strong sun or gentle rain?
What if a hardy weed intrudes?

<u>No matter; there's no dearth</u> —
<u>It mats the heath.</u>

<u>It thrives.</u>

Art Nouveau Dreams

PROLOGUE
Tell Me Something About Yourself

When my hair was cornsilk tassels
Down my back, disciplined to
Pigtails, and all the world
A big electric storm (not far,
Yet not too close; everything
Was loud enough to hear and bright
Enough to see) say, five miles away;
My mind was patterned like a piece of chintz,
Flower-shapes cluttering every inch of it,
And brighter where no light
Had touched to fade them, hid in folds
Where eight-year-old imagination holds
The best, most wonderful of secrets,
Secrets that were never really true:

There was a gnarled old lady of an apple tree
In my back yard, pretty only in the spring
With blossoming, but friendly always,
And smelling of sun on just-washed clothes.
There was an oak I trusted with my swing.
A dignified old deacon, was this oak;

It was like sitting in his lap for stories
To pump my swing and hear the whispers
Of the leaves in amiable reply to breezes,
A chance gust blew there; the big puffs
Of wind broke into fragmentary pieces
When they met the hard oldness of this oak.
I was not allowed to stand beneath the trees
If a storm should suddenly come close,

And I always ran for the house slowly as I could,
Feeling the worst deserter; waiting for the wood
To splinter from a lightning bolt that never came.

There was in the house that raised me
A cookie jar on the middle pantry shelf.
It kept its secrets well and nobody,
I was powerfully convinced, could tell
How many cookies went into a pocket after school—
They were such a spicy heap and surely, all uncounted?
The house that raised me was spotlit
With little sunlight-shafts of love, likewise uncounted,
So familiar they were hardly seen;
So deeply known as not to be forgotten now.

Tell me something about yourself.
Tell this person about the pantry shelf,
The swing hung from the patriarchal oak,
About the motion and the taste
Of a certain place, of a certain time?
It is impossible that one would know the place,
Or even just its name.

MARTHA

My grandmother was such a one—
A worker in the vineyards of the Lord,
But merry, merry as a May morning! –
And always ready with a lap for a tired child.
She had raised eight, lost three,
Yet never lost the wonder of a childseye view
When she regarded with her blazing gaze
The world around her, in continual flux,
Like all her children, and their children, too.
Her life spanned horse-drawn carriage
And the first jet-plane... and she embraced them both.
She polished all her silver spoons on Fridays,
And baked a kitchenfull of fragrance, Saturdays,
To celebrate the Sabbath, offer comfort,
Even though, as deaconess, she overrode
The radical proposal of cushions for the pews.
The congregation, she opined serenely,
Would hear the sermon clearer, seated firm
On rigid and uncompromising pews
Of rigid and uncompromising oak.
My grandmother gave me hugs and history;
Her hymnal is my heritage — but, also –
A comb of tortoise-shell that caught her auburn hair;
a little cameo that made her dress her own;
A pitcher with the colors of earth and sky;
A handstitched motto, overcoming all:
"THIS IS THE DAY THAT THE LORD HATH MADE:
LET US REJOICE IN IT AND BE GLAD."
I hope she knows: I try.

SUMMER SONG
For Patricia Lea Davis, 1959-85

When all the world's washed new again,
after the storm;
when breezes drenched with scent of rain
senses inform,
    then, that small brook beneath the bridge
    rolls toward its spill,
    and fills the lake, its primal pledge
    sworn to fulfill.
        The water wheel upon the verge
        turns and returns:
        what falls will rise; what floats, submerge
        —watching, one learns.
            That green, the color of our youth,
            color of hope, slips far beyond our mortal truth,
            out of our scope.
                But see the sunset sails afloat—
                Yes, mark them well!
                The Summer caught in one frail boat,
                riding the swell!

                On such does memory depend
                to turn Time's enemy to friend.

LITTLE NOCTURNE
The moon is falling low
Unlace your fingers from my hair,
And lift your cheek from mine,
And let your feet persuade you to the door.
But, if you can do none of these,
Then slip your arms about me, this once more,
Because you are not even gone before
I miss you more than I can bear.
The moon will rise again.

This is Jane Davis Carpenter's third collection of poetry. Two previous books were *Snapshots* and *Sightings*, both out of print. *Art Nouveau Dreams* is a more complete overview of her work.